Copyright

© 2024 Nidaash Consulting. All rights reserved.

This book is licensed for personal use only. No part of this publication may be reproduced, distributed, or transmitted in any form or by any means, including photocopying, recording, or other electronic or mechanical methods, without the prior written permission of the publisher, except for brief quotations in reviews or educational references. Unauthorized sharing, copying, or distribution of this work is strictly prohibited.

For permissions or inquiries, please contact info@nidaash.com

This publication is intended for informational purposes only. While every effort has been made to ensure accuracy, the author and publisher assume no responsibility for errors, omissions, or damages arising from the use of this material. Professional advice should be sought where appropriate.
Nidaash Consulting
www.nidaash.com

First Edition
Digital Edition
Published in India

Preface

Welcome to the second installment of the "HR on the Go" series, where we continue our journey through the essential components of human resource management. In our first topic, we laid the groundwork for effective recruitment strategies. Now, we turn our attention to talent acquisition, a crucial element that goes beyond merely filling positions; it involves strategically attracting, sourcing, and selecting the best talent to drive organizational success.

In today's competitive landscape, effective talent acquisition is more important than ever. Organizations must not only identify the right candidates but also ensure they align with company culture and values. This chapter will delve into the various facets of talent acquisition, including employer branding, candidate sourcing, selection processes, and the importance of data-driven decision-making.

Whether you're an experienced HR professional looking to refine your approach or new to the field and eager to learn, this chapter provides practical insights and actionable strategies to enhance your talent acquisition efforts. Each section is crafted to be concise and informative, making it easy to integrate these concepts into your daily practice without overwhelming your busy schedule.

Join me as we explore the dynamic world of talent acquisition and uncover the key processes and best practices that will help you attract and retain top talent in your organization. Together, we will build a robust understanding of talent acquisition that not only fills roles but also fosters a thriving workplace culture.

Introduction

Talent acquisition is more than just a function of human resources; it is a strategic endeavor that shapes the very foundation of an organization. In a world where the competition for skilled professionals is fierce, companies must develop a proactive approach to attract and retain the right talent. This chapter aims to illuminate the multifaceted nature of talent acquisition, exploring its significance in today's dynamic business environment.

Effective talent acquisition encompasses a range of activities, from building a compelling employer brand to employing innovative sourcing techniques. It requires a keen understanding of both the market and the organization's needs, enabling HR professionals to identify candidates who not only possess the requisite skills but also fit seamlessly into the company culture.

In this section, we will cover the core components of a successful talent acquisition strategy, including:

1. **Understanding Employer Branding**: How to position your organization as an employer of choice.

2. **Sourcing Candidates**: Techniques for identifying and engaging potential hires.

3. **Selection Processes**: Best practices for evaluating candidates and making informed hiring decisions.

4. **Data-Driven Talent Acquisition**: Utilizing analytics to enhance recruitment efforts and improve outcomes.

As we navigate through these topics, you will gain practical insights and tools that you can apply immediately to elevate your talent acquisition strategies. Whether you are an HR professional, a hiring manager, or a leader looking to optimize your workforce, this chapter will provide you with the knowledge necessary to build a strong pipeline of talent that aligns with your organization's goals.

Let's embark on this journey to unlock the secrets of effective talent acquisition and create a lasting impact on your organization's success.

Table of Contents

1. Understanding Talent Acquisition vs. Recruitment
2. Employer Branding & Employee Value Proposition (EVP)
3. Building Talent Pipelines & Forecasting Needs
4. Technology in Talent Acquisition: AI and Automation
5. Talent Acquisition Metrics & Data-Driven Decisions
6. Diversity, Equity & Inclusion (DEI) in Talent Acquisition
7. Global Talent Acquisition Strategies
8. Chapter: Acquiring Passive Talent
9. Talent Acquisition Case Studies and Exercises

Understanding Talent Acquisition vs. Recruitment

Introduction

In the world of Human Resources, terms like *recruitment* and *talent acquisition* are often used interchangeably, yet they represent different approaches to building a successful workforce. Recruitment is a short-term, task-driven process aimed at filling immediate vacancies, while talent acquisition is a strategic, ongoing approach focused on aligning talent with the company's long-term vision and objectives.

This chapter explores the fundamental differences between recruitment and talent acquisition, providing insights on how and when to apply each approach to optimize the hiring process and better meet the organization's needs.

Defining Recruitment and Talent Acquisition

Recruitment

Recruitment is the immediate, tactical process of attracting, screening, and hiring suitable candidates for a specific position. It typically follows a reactive model—initiating the process when a vacancy arises. Recruitment is often characterized by a sequence of activities, such as posting job ads, screening resumes, interviewing candidates, and making an offer.

- **Primary Goal**: Fill vacancies as they arise.
- **Approach**: Transactional and time-sensitive.
- **Outcome**: Immediate hiring to address short-term staffing needs.

Talent Acquisition

Talent acquisition, on the other hand, is a strategic, proactive, and long-term process. It involves building a talent pipeline that aligns with the organization's future workforce needs and growth strategy. Talent acquisition encompasses not only recruitment but also employer branding, workforce planning, and relationship-building with potential candidates.

- **Primary Goal**: Develop a steady talent pipeline to fulfill future needs.
- **Approach**: Strategic, ongoing, and proactive.
- **Outcome**: Sustainable talent pool for future positions and long-term business growth.

1.3. Key Differences Between Recruitment and Talent Acquisition

Aspect	Recruitment	Talent Acquisition
Focus	Immediate hiring needs	Long-term talent pipeline
Approach	Reactive and transactional	Proactive and strategic
Time Horizon	Short-term	Long-term
Employer Branding	Limited focus on brand	Emphasis on branding and employee value proposition
Candidate Relationships	Minimal interaction beyond hiring process	Building ongoing relationships with potential candidates
Metrics	Time-to-fill, cost-per-hire	Quality of hire, talent pipeline strength

Why Talent Acquisition Matters in Today's Workforce?

Aligning with Organizational Goals
Talent acquisition aligns hiring practices with broader

organizational goals, ensuring that the talent brought in supports growth strategies. For example, if a tech company plans to expand into AI and machine learning, talent acquisition will proactively focus on identifying and engaging with experts in those fields well before a vacancy arises.

Building a Competitive Advantage

In competitive markets, finding top talent before competitors is a crucial advantage. Talent acquisition allows organizations to tap into passive candidates—those who may not actively seek jobs but are interested in engaging with a company over time.

Employer Branding

A robust talent acquisition strategy emphasizes employer branding, creating a positive reputation in the job market. Candidates are increasingly looking for organizations with strong values, commitment to employee growth, and work-life balance. Talent acquisition helps craft this brand, making the organization a preferred choice among potential employees.

Flexibility in Changing Markets

Talent acquisition provides the flexibility to adapt to changes in the job market. For instance, if there's a shift towards remote work or specific skills become scarce, talent acquisition can pivot to address these trends, ensuring that the organization remains resilient and adaptable.

1.5. Example Scenarios: Recruitment vs. Talent Acquisition

Scenario 1: Immediate Hiring Need (Recruitment)

A retail company experiences a surge in customers during the holiday season, requiring additional staff at short notice. The HR team initiates recruitment to fill cashier, sales associate, and stockroom positions. The goal here is to quickly hire seasonal workers for a limited period.

- **Action**: Recruiters post job ads, conduct interviews, and make quick hires.
- **Outcome**: Positions are filled promptly to meet the seasonal demand.

Scenario 2: Long-Term Workforce Planning (Talent Acquisition)

A software development company foresees the need for cloud computing engineers as it expands its services over the next few years. The HR team develops a talent acquisition strategy to attract top talent in cloud computing through internships, university partnerships, and by establishing the company as a desirable place for tech talent.

- **Action**: HR engages in branding initiatives, establishes relationships with tech communities, and starts building a talent pool.
- **Outcome**: The company has a pool of qualified candidates ready when the need arises, reducing time-to-fill and increasing quality of hire.

Developing a Talent Acquisition Strategy

Workforce Planning

Identify the skills and competencies needed to achieve long-term business goals. This involves understanding future hiring requirements based on growth projections and market trends.

Employer Branding

Create an employer brand that resonates with potential candidates. Communicate what makes the company a desirable place to work, highlighting values, mission, and culture.

Building Talent Pipelines

Establish relationships with potential candidates even when there are no immediate job openings. This may include networking, engagement on social media, attending industry events, and creating an alumni network for previous employees.

Data-Driven Decision-Making

Leverage data analytics to gain insights into hiring trends, candidate preferences, and talent availability. Use metrics like quality of hire and pipeline strength to assess the effectiveness of the talent acquisition strategy.

Nurturing Relationships with Passive Candidates

Passive candidates are often top-performing professionals who are not actively seeking new positions. Engaging with them through regular communication, thought leadership content, and personalized updates keeps the organization on their radar for future opportunities.

Exercises

Exercise 1: Distinguishing Between Recruitment and Talent Acquisition

1. Identify a recent hiring need within your organization and determine if it was handled through recruitment or talent acquisition.
2. List three actions taken during the hiring process and assess if they aligned more with a short-term recruitment approach or a strategic talent acquisition strategy.
3. Consider how this approach could have been adapted to better align with the organization's long-term goals.

Exercise 2: Creating a Talent Acquisition Strategy for a Key Role

1. Choose a role that will be critical for your organization in the coming years (e.g., data analyst, digital marketing specialist).
2. Develop a talent acquisition strategy for this role, outlining the following:
    - Branding initiatives to attract candidates.
    - Potential partnerships (universities, industry organizations).
    - Engagement methods to build relationships with passive candidates.
3. Identify at least three key metrics you would use to measure the success of this strategy.

Exercise 3: Employer Branding Assessment

1. Evaluate your organization's current employer brand. Consider online reviews, social media presence, and candidate feedback.
2. Identify any gaps or areas where the brand could be strengthened to attract quality candidates.
3. Develop a plan to address these gaps, focusing on key attributes that make the organization an appealing place to work.

1.8. Conclusion

Understanding the distinctions between recruitment and talent acquisition empowers HR professionals to approach hiring with both a short-term and long-term mindset. While recruitment focuses on immediate hiring needs, talent acquisition is a proactive, strategic approach that builds a sustainable talent pipeline aligned with organizational goals. With a strong talent acquisition strategy, companies can not only fill immediate vacancies but also future-proof their workforce by attracting high-quality candidates well before positions open.

By the end of this chapter, you should be able to differentiate between recruitment and talent acquisition, understand when to apply each approach, and begin developing a talent acquisition strategy that positions your organization for long-term success.

Employer Branding & Employee Value Proposition (EVP)

Introduction

Employer branding has become a critical element in the competitive talent landscape, helping organizations differentiate themselves as employers of choice. More than just recruiting, it's about crafting a strong, consistent image and reputation that resonates with top talent and aligns with the company's mission, vision, and values. Closely tied to employer branding is the Employee Value Proposition (EVP)—a unique set of benefits and experiences an organization offers employees in exchange for their skills and loyalty.

Understanding and leveraging both employer branding and EVP can significantly impact talent acquisition and retention, influencing everything from applicant quality to long-term employee engagement. This chapter explores these concepts in detail, providing steps to build a compelling brand and EVP.

What is Employer Branding?

Employer branding is the strategic process by which an organization showcases itself to attract, engage, and retain talent. It's about creating a clear and consistent narrative about what it's like to work for the organization. This brand identity encompasses various aspects, such as company culture, career development opportunities, and work-life balance, giving potential employees a realistic picture of the organization's values and day-to-day experience.

Unlike EVP, which focuses on the specific offerings for employees, employer branding is the broader, outward-facing image that potential candidates see. This includes how the company interacts on social media, the stories it shares about employee experiences, and the values it highlights to the public.

Understanding the Employee Value Proposition (EVP)

The EVP is the promise a company makes to its employees. It's the "give and get" equation that defines the unique benefits, growth opportunities, and rewards employees receive in exchange for their efforts. A strong EVP not only draws high-quality candidates but also fosters loyalty, as it provides a compelling reason for employees to stay and contribute to the organization's success.

While employer branding creates the external perception, the EVP is the internal foundation that fuels this perception. A well-defined EVP outlines the specific tangible and intangible rewards that make working at the organization unique, such as professional development, a supportive culture, competitive compensation, and work-life balance.

The Difference Between Employer Branding and EVP

Employer branding and EVP are interconnected but serve distinct roles. Employer branding is the external image projected to the job market, while the EVP is the internal offer made to employees. Together, they create a cohesive identity, presenting the organization as a desirable place to work and fostering engagement and loyalty among current employees.

For instance, a tech company known for innovation might emphasize a cutting-edge work environment and opportunities for creative experimentation as part of its brand. Its EVP, in turn, could offer benefits like flexible work schedules, professional development programs in emerging technologies, and a culture that encourages innovation. In this way, the employer brand and EVP align to attract professionals drawn to such a dynamic environment.

Building a Strong Employer Brand

Creating a strong employer brand goes beyond a catchy slogan or campaign; it requires a clear understanding of the organization's values, mission, and what makes it unique to employees. Authentic employee stories are a powerful tool in employer branding, offering real-life examples of career growth, team achievements, and daily experiences that bring the brand to life.

Awards, diversity initiatives, and employee success stories featured on social media, the company's website, and at recruiting events can further solidify the brand's message. Regularly sharing these highlights keeps the brand relevant and demonstrates the organization's commitment to an engaging, inclusive, and supportive work environment.

Developing an Authentic EVP

A compelling EVP is built from the inside out and should reflect what current employees value most about the organization. Employee feedback is invaluable in crafting an EVP that truly resonates; regular surveys and feedback sessions help uncover what employees find rewarding and what could improve. An EVP might include competitive salaries, career advancement opportunities, purposeful work, a supportive culture, and a healthy work-life balance.

Once the EVP is established, it's essential to communicate it consistently both internally and externally. The EVP must be woven into all aspects of the employee lifecycle, from onboarding and performance management to learning and development. This ensures that the EVP is not only attractive to potential candidates but also reinforces loyalty among current employees.

Case Study: Employer Branding and EVP in Practice

Consider the example of a consulting firm aiming to attract professionals who prioritize career growth and meaningful work. Their employer brand might focus on mentorship programs, challenging client projects, and a clear career path for advancement. Their EVP would support this by offering competitive salaries, professional certifications, and regular promotions. The alignment of brand and EVP creates a clear value proposition, appealing to candidates looking for a challenging and rewarding environment.

In this way, both current and future employees see the organization as a place where they can thrive professionally and personally, reinforcing the brand and reducing turnover as employees find long-term value within the company.

Leveraging Data to Refine Branding and EVP

Data analytics provide valuable insights into employer branding and EVP effectiveness. Monitoring employee reviews on platforms like Glassdoor, analyzing social media engagement, and conducting exit interviews help organizations understand how their brand is perceived and how it might be improved. For instance, if employees highly value flexibility, this could be integrated into the EVP through remote work options, flexible hours, or wellness programs.

Using data to continually assess and adjust branding efforts ensures that the company stays aligned with market trends and employee expectations, making the organization adaptable to the changing workforce landscape.

The Impact of a Strong Employer Brand and EVP

A well-aligned employer brand and EVP create a ripple effect throughout the organization. Attracting a steady stream of qualified candidates, improving employee satisfaction, and fostering a culture that reflects the organization's values all contribute to lower turnover rates and higher engagement levels. For both prospective and current employees, the company becomes more than just a workplace; it becomes a space for growth, contribution, and meaningful experiences.

In today's competitive job market, organizations that can effectively convey their brand and EVP stand out as employers of choice, attracting and retaining talent that aligns with their mission and values. A consistent, authentic employer brand, backed by a well-defined EVP, builds a resilient identity that evolves alongside industry demands and workforce trends.

Exercises

Exercise 1: Assessing Your Employer Brand

1. Conduct an audit of your current employer brand by reviewing how the organization presents itself on social media, job boards, and employee review sites.
2. Gather feedback from employees on what they believe makes the organization unique and appealing.
3. Summarize your findings, highlighting strengths and potential areas for improvement in your branding.

Exercise 2: Crafting an EVP Statement

1. List the unique benefits and opportunities your organization offers, focusing on culture, growth, and work environment.
2. Identify areas of alignment with what top candidates in your industry seek in an employer.
3. Draft a clear EVP statement that captures the organization's unique value for current and potential employees.

Exercise 3: Telling Your Employer Story

1. Identify a few employees whose stories exemplify the organization's culture and values.
2. Interview them to create authentic stories about their experiences, growth, or memorable projects.
3. Publish these stories on your careers page or social media to bring the brand to life for potential hires.

Exercise 4: Employee Feedback and EVP Adjustment

1. Use a survey or interview feedback to gather input on the current EVP and identify any gaps.
2. Adjust the EVP to address these findings, focusing on benefits and experiences employees value most.
3. Develop a plan to communicate the EVP more effectively within the organization.

Exercise 5: Competitor Benchmarking

1. Research the employer brands and EVPs of two to three competitors.
2. Identify unique elements that make their employer branding and EVP effective.
3. Brainstorm ways to differentiate your organization's brand and EVP, adding any new ideas for improvement.

Conclusion

Employer branding and EVP are essential tools for attracting and retaining talent in today's dynamic market. By crafting a compelling employer brand and a well-aligned EVP, organizations can position themselves as employers of choice, creating a culture of loyalty, engagement, and shared values. With consistent messaging, authentic storytelling, and data-driven refinement, companies can build a resilient brand that stands out and adapts to meet the demands of an ever-evolving workforce.

Building Talent Pipelines & Forecasting Needs

Introduction

In today's fast-paced talent landscape, organizations must be proactive rather than reactive in their recruitment efforts. Building a talent pipeline—a pool of pre-qualified, engaged candidates ready to fill future roles—helps companies prepare for growth, minimize the impact of turnover, and align talent acquisition with long-term business goals. This approach is complemented by workforce forecasting, which anticipates future hiring needs based on factors like business expansion, project requirements, and market trends. Together, talent pipelines and forecasting create a strategic foundation for sustained, agile talent acquisition.

This chapter will explore the components of building a talent pipeline and the steps involved in workforce forecasting, with practical examples to illustrate how companies can effectively leverage these strategies.

What is a Talent Pipeline?

A talent pipeline is more than just a list of potential candidates; it's a structured approach to identifying, engaging, and nurturing individuals who may fill roles in the future. Rather than waiting until there's an immediate opening, HR teams proactively connect with both active and passive candidates who may be interested in joining the organization at a later date.

Example: Imagine a growing healthcare provider anticipating an increased demand for qualified nurses in the coming years. To build a pipeline, the HR team attends nursing school job fairs, engages with alumni networks, and maintains relationships with nursing students and recent graduates. By doing so, they create a pool of potential candidates who could quickly step into open roles when needed, reducing time-to-hire.

Key Components of an Effective Talent Pipeline

An effective talent pipeline requires careful planning and ongoing maintenance. Here are several core components involved in building a successful pipeline:

- **Role Clarity**: Identify and prioritize roles essential to business growth. This allows HR teams to focus on recruiting individuals with skill sets aligned with these positions.

- **Sourcing Strategy**: Engage multiple channels to identify potential candidates. Platforms like LinkedIn, niche job boards, professional networking events, and employee referrals provide access to a wide, diverse range of qualified candidates.

  Example: A software development company might source developers through GitHub (a platform where developers showcase their code) or attend hackathons to meet professionals with specialized programming skills.

- **Engagement and Relationship-Building**: Cultivate relationships with candidates, even when there isn't an immediate job opening. This includes sharing valuable content, such as industry updates or company news, to keep candidates engaged.

  Example: A marketing firm that frequently hires creative talent might stay connected with promising candidates through a quarterly newsletter sharing insights on current marketing trends, which keeps the company top-of-mind.

- **Pipeline Segmentation**: Organize candidates by skill set, experience level, or role type for easier access when hiring needs arise.

- **Tracking and Management**: Utilize an Applicant Tracking System (ATS) or Customer Relationship Management (CRM) software to maintain candidate records, track engagement, and segment candidates effectively. This way, HR teams can easily access the right candidates as roles open up.

Understanding Workforce Forecasting

Workforce forecasting is the practice of predicting future talent needs. This process requires analyzing both internal data, like historical hiring trends and employee turnover rates, and external data, such as industry labor market trends. Forecasting allows organizations to prepare for anticipated growth or contractions in their workforce, helping align recruiting efforts with business goals.

Example: A retail company may anticipate higher hiring needs before the holiday season due to increased customer traffic. By forecasting these needs, the company can begin building its talent pipeline several months in advance, reducing the need for urgent, last-minute hires.

Steps to Build a Talent Pipeline and Forecasting Needs

Step 1: Define Critical Roles and Competencies

Identify roles crucial to business success, focusing on positions that significantly impact productivity, revenue, or customer satisfaction. Collaborate with department heads to understand both current and future needs, as well as the specific competencies required.

Example: A logistics company with rapid growth might define its critical roles as warehouse supervisors and inventory managers. Knowing the technical skills and certifications required for these roles allows HR to target the right talent.

Step 2: Create a Candidate Persona

Develop a profile for each role that outlines the ideal candidate's skills, experience, and cultural fit. This helps in targeting candidates who not only meet technical requirements but also align with company values and work styles.

Example: For a high-impact sales role, a company might create a persona that includes qualities like strong communication skills, resilience, and previous sales experience in a high-volume environment.

Step 3: Proactively Source Candidates

Identify candidates through various sourcing methods, including social media, employee referrals, and professional networks. Additionally, use recruitment marketing strategies like thought leadership articles, webinars, and social media posts to attract passive candidates who may not be actively looking for a job but could be interested in future opportunities.

Example: A consulting firm might publish industry insights on LinkedIn to showcase its expertise and attract candidates who resonate with its thought leadership, nurturing a pipeline of individuals likely to be interested in future consulting roles.

Step 4: Engage and Nurture Relationships

Regular engagement is essential to maintain relationships with potential candidates. This could involve sending occasional updates on the company's achievements, inviting candidates to events, or even recognizing milestones like work anniversaries.

These touchpoints help keep candidates engaged and deepen their connection to the company.

Example: A tech startup with high demand for data scientists might periodically send research findings or updates about new technologies they're using. This engagement reinforces the company's brand and appeals to candidates interested in cutting-edge innovation.

Step 5: Conduct Workforce Forecasting

Using historical data and market insights, project future hiring needs. Consider factors like business expansion, seasonal spikes, and anticipated employee turnover. Forecasting allows HR teams to be prepared with talent pipelines tailored to specific timelines and demand.

Example: A call center anticipating increased staffing needs for a product launch might analyze previous product releases, forecasting the number of customer support representatives needed and building a pipeline of candidates ready for training.

Step 6: Review and Adjust Regularly

Regularly evaluate the pipeline's effectiveness, gathering feedback from hiring managers and analyzing data on hires made from the pipeline. Adjust sourcing strategies and engagement methods as needed to ensure the pipeline remains relevant and effective.

Example: A financial services company might realize that candidates sourced from online finance forums have higher retention rates. Based on this insight, they focus more efforts on sourcing from these forums while adjusting less effective sourcing channels.

Case Study: Talent Pipeline and Forecasting in Action

A global e-commerce company with fluctuating demand based on seasonality offers a clear example of talent pipeline management and forecasting. Anticipating a surge in customer inquiries during the holiday season, the company's HR team uses past data to project the number of additional customer support representatives needed. Starting in July, they build a pipeline of candidates through virtual hiring events, social media campaigns, and local job fairs. By maintaining regular contact with candidates and conducting a training program in October, they ensure these employees are ready for a smooth onboarding by November. As a result, the company meets its seasonal demand without disruption.

Using Technology in Talent Pipeline and Forecasting

Technology plays a crucial role in pipeline building and forecasting, offering tools that streamline processes and enhance accuracy. Applicant Tracking Systems (ATS) and Customer Relationship Management (CRM) platforms help track candidate interactions, monitor engagement, and manage segmented talent pools. Workforce analytics tools provide insights into turnover rates, hiring patterns, and industry benchmarks, helping organizations refine forecasting over time.

Example: A manufacturing company might use predictive analytics to determine that production line managers tend to stay in their roles for an average of three years. Armed with this insight, the HR team can begin building a pipeline of potential candidates well in advance of expected openings.

Benefits of Building Talent Pipelines and Forecasting Needs

A well-maintained talent pipeline and accurate forecasting provide numerous benefits:

- **Reduced Time-to-Hire**: Having a pool of pre-qualified candidates accelerates hiring when roles become available.
- **Higher Candidate Quality**: By building relationships with top talent, companies improve the likelihood of hiring well-matched candidates.
- **Cost Efficiency**: Proactive recruitment reduces the expenses associated with last-minute hires and temporary staffing solutions.
- **Strategic Alignment**: Forecasting ensures that recruiting efforts are aligned with business objectives, allowing organizations to scale efficiently and adapt to changes.

Exercises

Exercise 1: Define a Talent Pipeline for a High-Impact Role

1. Choose a key role within your organization that requires a steady flow of qualified candidates.
2. Identify three sourcing channels you'll use to find candidates and list engagement strategies to keep these candidates interested over time.

Exercise 2: Create a Candidate Persona for Pipeline Building

1. Develop a candidate persona for a role in your pipeline, detailing key skills, experience, and cultural fit.
2. Based on this persona, list three methods to source candidates that fit this profile.

Exercise 3: Conduct Workforce Forecasting for an Upcoming Project

1. Analyze an upcoming project and determine the roles needed to support it.

2. Forecast the anticipated start date, skills required, and number of hires needed. Develop a timeline for when pipeline-building should begin.

Exercise 4: Engage Talent Pipeline Candidates

1. Develop a quarterly engagement plan for potential candidates, including content ideas such as company updates, industry news, or invitations to webinars.
2. Track engagement levels to determine which methods yield the best response and adjust accordingly.

Exercise 5: Measure Pipeline Effectiveness and Adjust

1. Set up a quarterly review to assess the effectiveness of your talent pipeline, tracking hires made, candidate engagement, and any challenges encountered.
2. Gather feedback from hiring managers on the quality of candidates in the pipeline and adjust sourcing or engagement strategies as needed.

Conclusion

Building a talent pipeline and forecasting hiring needs are foundational steps for proactive, strategic recruitment. A well-managed pipeline ensures that organizations have qualified candidates readily available, while forecasting helps align hiring efforts with organizational goals. Together, these strategies enable companies to adapt quickly, reduce time-to-hire, and maintain a steady flow of top talent aligned with long-term objectives.

Technology in Talent Acquisition: AI and Automation

Introduction

The rise of artificial intelligence (AI) and automation in talent acquisition has transformed how companies recruit and manage candidates, streamlining workflows and allowing HR professionals to focus on strategic initiatives. From initial screening to onboarding, AI-powered tools and automated systems are reshaping each phase of recruitment, driving efficiency and accuracy. However, leveraging these technologies requires careful planning to align with organizational goals and maintain ethical standards.

This chapter will explore the key applications of AI and automation in recruitment, discussing the benefits, challenges, and ethical considerations. We will look at real-world examples to illustrate best practices and end with exercises to help you think strategically about integrating these tools into your own recruitment process.

The Role of AI and Automation in Talent Acquisition

Artificial Intelligence (AI) refers to the use of advanced algorithms and machine learning models to perform tasks that mimic human intelligence, such as problem-solving, decision-making, and language understanding. In talent acquisition, AI helps process large amounts of data, identify patterns, and make predictions, allowing HR teams to make data-driven decisions.

Automation, on the other hand, involves using technology to execute repetitive tasks without human intervention. When applied to recruitment, automation can handle routine tasks like resume screening, interview scheduling, and candidate communications, freeing up HR professionals to focus on relationship-building and strategic decision-making.

Applications of AI and Automation in Recruitment

1. Resume Screening and Shortlisting

One of the most time-consuming tasks in recruitment is screening hundreds or thousands of resumes to find candidates who meet the required qualifications. AI tools can analyze resumes and cover letters, identifying relevant skills, experience, and qualifications based on predefined criteria.

Example: A large e-commerce company using an AI-based resume screening tool reduces its time spent reviewing applications by 70%. The tool is programmed to identify specific keywords related to the required skills, certifications, and experience levels. As a result, recruiters receive a pre-screened, ranked list of qualified candidates, enabling them to focus on high-potential applicants.

2. Candidate Matching

AI-powered candidate matching tools analyze job descriptions and compare them with resumes to assess compatibility. These tools often use natural language processing (NLP) to match not just keywords but also related skills and experience levels, resulting in a more accurate shortlist of candidates.

Example: A healthcare organization looking to hire nurses uses an AI-driven candidate matching system to identify candidates with the specific certifications required for each department. By examining job description nuances, such as experience with certain patient demographics, the AI tool narrows down the list to individuals who best align with the organization's needs.

3. Chatbots for Candidate Engagement

AI chatbots are increasingly popular in recruitment, offering a quick and efficient way to engage candidates. Chatbots can answer frequently asked questions, schedule interviews, collect application details, and provide real-time feedback. This instant interaction keeps candidates engaged, improves their experience, and saves recruiters time.

Example: A multinational technology firm implements an AI chatbot on its career page. The chatbot greets visitors, answers questions about job openings, and helps candidates apply for relevant roles. If a candidate has already applied, the chatbot updates them on the application status, enhancing transparency and engagement.

4. Predictive Analytics for Talent Forecasting

Predictive analytics uses historical data and statistical algorithms to forecast future recruitment needs. By analyzing factors like employee turnover, promotion patterns, and market trends, predictive analytics helps organizations anticipate talent needs and prepare pipelines in advance.

Example: A logistics company with seasonal demand uses predictive analytics to forecast staffing needs. Based on past data, it anticipates a surge in demand for warehouse staff in the lead-up to the holiday season. Armed with this information, the HR team proactively recruits and onboards temporary workers, ensuring a smooth operation during peak periods.

5. Automated Interview Scheduling

Coordinating interviews can be a logistical challenge, especially for roles with multiple rounds or involving multiple interviewers. Automated scheduling tools streamline this process by allowing candidates to choose from available time slots, syncing with recruiters' and interviewers' calendars, and sending reminders.
Example: A financial services firm struggling with no-shows and scheduling delays implements an automated interview scheduling tool. Candidates receive a personalized link to select an interview slot, reducing back-and-forth emails. Automated

reminders decrease the no-show rate, improving efficiency and candidate experience.

6. Bias Reduction in Hiring

AI can help reduce unconscious bias in recruitment by evaluating candidates based solely on qualifications and performance indicators. While not infallible, these systems are designed to mitigate bias by focusing on objective criteria, thus fostering a more inclusive hiring process.

Example: A media company using an AI-driven tool for resume screening ensures that resumes are reviewed based on skills and experience alone, with personal details like names and locations anonymized. This approach helps reduce potential bias and promotes a fairer hiring process.

Challenges and Ethical Considerations in AI and Automation

While AI and automation offer clear benefits, they also raise important ethical and operational challenges:

- **Data Privacy**: AI tools rely on large amounts of data, raising concerns over the security and privacy of candidate information. Organizations must comply with data protection regulations, like the GDPR, to safeguard personal information.
- **Bias in Algorithms**: AI is only as unbiased as the data it's trained on. If historical hiring data reflects biases, AI tools may inadvertently reinforce them. Regular audits and diverse data inputs are essential to minimize bias.
- **Human Touch**: Over-reliance on automation can make recruitment feel impersonal. While AI handles many tasks, recruiters should maintain a human touch in interactions that influence candidate perception and experience.

- **Accuracy and Transparency**: Candidates may have concerns about how AI tools evaluate them. It's important to be transparent about AI use and ensure that algorithms are fair, accurate, and align with organizational values.

Example of Ethical Dilemmas: A global consulting firm introduced an AI-driven recruitment tool to screen candidates but later found that it disproportionately favored candidates from specific educational backgrounds, reflecting biases in its training data. The firm reassessed the algorithm, adjusted data inputs, and introduced regular audits to ensure fairer candidate selection.

Steps to Implement AI and Automation in Talent Acquisition

Step 1: Identify Key Pain Points in the Recruitment Process

Start by identifying bottlenecks in your recruitment process, such as time-consuming resume reviews or frequent candidate drop-offs. Understanding where AI or automation can add value helps tailor solutions to your specific needs.

Example: A retail chain facing a high turnover rate uses AI to analyze exit interviews and turnover data, identifying patterns and improving candidate screening for high-turnover roles.

Step 2: Choose the Right AI and Automation Tools
Selecting tools that align with your goals is critical. Evaluate various options and choose those that best meet your requirements, considering factors like ease of integration, customization, and vendor support.

Step 3: Train and Prepare Your Team

Introducing AI and automation requires upskilling recruiters and HR staff. Ensure your team understands the tools and feels comfortable using them, focusing on how AI complements their roles rather than replacing them.

Step 4: Regularly Monitor and Adjust

To maximize effectiveness, continuously monitor the performance of AI and automation tools. Conduct regular reviews, solicit feedback from users, and make adjustments to improve accuracy and fairness.

Benefits of AI and Automation in Talent Acquisition

- **Efficiency**: AI reduces the time spent on repetitive tasks, allowing HR teams to focus on higher-value activities.
- **Improved Candidate Experience**: Automated responses and streamlined processes enhance candidate engagement and satisfaction.
- **Cost Savings**: AI can reduce recruitment costs by accelerating hiring and decreasing the need for external hiring agencies.
- **Data-Driven Decisions**: AI tools provide actionable insights, enabling data-backed decisions on candidate selection, engagement, and forecasting.

Exercises

Exercise 1: Identify Automation Opportunities
1. Review your current recruitment workflow and list five tasks that are repetitive and time-consuming.
2. For each task, consider how automation could improve efficiency or effectiveness.

Exercise 2: Ethical AI Assessment
1. Choose an AI tool (real or hypothetical) used for candidate screening.
2. Identify potential biases that could arise from using this tool and suggest ways to mitigate these biases.

Exercise 3: Predictive Analytics Application
1. Use data from a recent hiring cycle to predict your organization's future hiring needs for a particular role.
2. Based on this analysis, develop a timeline for building a talent pipeline for this role.

Exercise 4: Developing an AI-based Candidate Persona
1. Identify a high-turnover role within your organization.
2. Use AI to analyze characteristics of successful employees in this role and create a data-driven candidate persona.

Exercise 5: Map Candidate Engagement Using Automation
1. Map the candidate journey from application to onboarding.
2. Identify where automation, such as email sequences or chatbots, could enhance candidate engagement, and create a basic plan.

Conclusion

The integration of AI and automation in talent acquisition has revolutionized recruitment, providing HR teams with powerful tools to streamline processes, engage candidates, and improve hiring quality. By effectively implementing these technologies, organizations can not only enhance efficiency but also gain a competitive edge in attracting top talent. As we continue to embrace digital transformation in HR, the key lies in balancing technology with the human touch, ensuring ethical practices, and adapting to ever-evolving candidate expectations. Through careful planning and ethical considerations, companies can harness the full potential of AI and automation to drive meaningful, long-term success in talent acquisition.

Talent Acquisition Metrics & Data-Driven Decisions

Introduction

Talent acquisition has evolved from traditional, intuition-based hiring practices to a data-driven discipline. Organizations increasingly rely on talent acquisition metrics to evaluate the efficiency and effectiveness of their recruitment processes. These metrics not only provide insight into how well recruitment goals are being met but also support data-driven decision-making that aligns hiring strategies with broader organizational objectives.

This chapter explores essential talent acquisition metrics and demonstrates how data analysis can transform recruitment practices. We'll cover key metrics to track, discuss their impact, and share examples to illustrate how data can guide better decisions. Finally, exercises will help you evaluate and refine your metrics for strategic advantage.

Key Talent Acquisition Metrics

1. Time to Fill

Time to Fill measures the duration between a job requisition and the acceptance of an offer. This metric reflects the efficiency of the recruitment process and is crucial for roles requiring quick replacements to avoid productivity loss.

Example: A manufacturing company tracks time to fill for its production line roles, which tend to have high turnover. When time to fill exceeds a target of 30 days, HR reviews the sourcing strategy to identify bottlenecks, ultimately implementing a new partnership with trade schools to accelerate hiring.

2. Cost per Hire

Cost per Hire aggregates all costs associated with filling a position, including advertising, recruiter salaries, travel, and onboarding. Monitoring this metric allows organizations to optimize budgets and justify recruitment expenses.

Example: A startup discovers that its cost per hire for senior engineering roles is significantly higher than budgeted. Upon analysis, they find that high travel costs for onsite interviews contribute to the increase. By adopting virtual interviews, they reduce travel expenses and bring cost per hire within target range.

3. Quality of Hire

Quality of Hire assesses the value a new employee brings to the organization, typically measured by performance ratings, retention rates, and cultural fit. This metric reflects the effectiveness of sourcing and selection processes in attracting top talent.

Example: A tech company compares the first-year performance scores of employees sourced from different channels. Candidates hired through employee referrals receive higher performance ratings, prompting the company to increase investment in its referral program.

4. Candidate Experience

Candidate Experience evaluates how positively candidates perceive the recruitment process, often measured through surveys post-interview or post-hire. Improving candidate experience can boost employer branding and conversion rates.

Example: A financial institution surveys candidates who declined offers to uncover factors influencing their decisions. Feedback highlights long wait times for interview feedback as a pain point, leading the organization to streamline communications, resulting in higher acceptance rates.

5. Offer Acceptance Rate

Offer Acceptance Rate is the percentage of job offers accepted by candidates. A low acceptance rate may signal issues with compensation, work culture, or competition, highlighting areas for improvement.

Example: An e-commerce company experiences a declining offer acceptance rate in a competitive market. To counter this, they conduct market research to reassess their compensation packages and enhance benefits, subsequently improving acceptance rates.

6. Diversity Metrics

Diversity metrics measure the proportion of hires from underrepresented groups, helping organizations foster a more inclusive workplace. Monitoring these metrics supports diverse hiring strategies and compliance with equal opportunity guidelines.

Example: A global corporation aims to increase gender diversity in its engineering teams. By tracking diversity metrics and partnering with organizations that support women in STEM, they achieve a 10% increase in female hires over a year.

7. Recruitment Funnel Metrics

Recruitment funnel metrics track each stage of the hiring process, from sourcing to offer acceptance. Common funnel metrics include *Application to Interview Rate*, *Interview to Offer Rate*, and *Offer to Hire Rate*. Analyzing these rates identifies where candidates drop off and where process improvements are needed.

Example: A consulting firm analyzes its funnel and finds that many candidates drop out after the interview stage due to prolonged decision times. By prioritizing faster feedback, they improve the interview-to-offer conversion rate.

Data-Driven Decision-Making in Talent Acquisition

Talent acquisition metrics enable HR leaders to make informed decisions based on quantitative data, leading to more consistent and measurable improvements.

Optimizing Sourcing Channels

By examining which channels produce the highest quality hires, organizations can allocate resources effectively. A data-driven approach helps eliminate low-performing channels and increase focus on sources with better returns.

Example: A retail brand finds that social media advertising drives high application volume but low conversion rates. Shifting focus to specialized job boards for retail professionals yields better-qualified candidates.

Predicting Workforce Needs

Forecasting future hiring needs with metrics such as historical turnover rates, seasonal demand, and employee growth supports proactive recruitment planning.

Example: A logistics company uses historical turnover data and seasonal demand analysis to anticipate peak hiring needs, allowing them to build a talent pool well in advance.

Improving Diversity and Inclusion

By tracking diversity metrics, organizations can identify underrepresented groups in their hiring processes and take proactive steps to enhance inclusivity. This data can inform initiatives, partnerships, and tailored recruitment strategies.

Example: A tech firm seeking to improve racial diversity in technical roles collaborates with universities and diversity-focused job boards, resulting in increased applications from diverse candidates.

Steps for Implementing Data-Driven Talent Acquisition

Step 1: Define Goals and Relevant Metrics

Start by identifying recruitment goals, such as reducing time to fill, increasing diversity, or enhancing candidate experience. Select metrics that align with these objectives, ensuring they provide clear insight into progress.

Example: A hospitality chain facing high turnover aims to improve quality of hire by focusing on retention rates of new hires. They adopt a metric that tracks the six-month retention rate to evaluate hiring success.

Step 2: Collect and Analyze Data

Gather data from applicant tracking systems (ATS), candidate surveys, and performance reviews to create a holistic view of your talent acquisition effectiveness. Use analytical tools to identify patterns and areas for improvement.

Step 3: Benchmark Metrics and Set Targets

Compare your metrics against industry benchmarks to set realistic targets and track progress over time. Benchmarking helps ensure your efforts align with industry standards and competitive pressures.

Step 4: Act on Insights and Refine Metrics

Based on data insights, take corrective actions to optimize recruitment processes. Regularly review and adjust your metrics as business needs evolve, ensuring continuous improvement.

Examples of Data-Driven Decisions in Action

Improving Time to Fill: A pharmaceutical company with extended time-to-fill cycles leverages data to identify delays in the approval process. By empowering hiring managers with faster decision-making tools, they reduce time to fill by 20%.

Enhancing Candidate Experience: A software company using candidate experience surveys discovers dissatisfaction with the lengthy assessment process. By streamlining assessments and providing timely updates, they increase candidate satisfaction and reduce drop-off rates.

Increasing Quality of Hire: An energy firm finds that candidates from specific universities tend to perform better in technical roles. They adjust their sourcing strategy to focus on partnerships with these institutions, improving the overall quality of hires.

Benefits of Using Talent Acquisition Metrics

- **Enhanced Decision-Making**: Metrics provide a factual basis for strategic decisions, reducing reliance on intuition.

- **Improved Efficiency**: Tracking and analyzing metrics reveal process inefficiencies, enabling corrective measures to streamline recruitment.

- **Stronger Employer Branding**: Metrics around candidate experience and satisfaction allow organizations to enhance their employer brand by refining interactions.
- **Increased Accountability**: Metrics set measurable targets for recruitment teams, fostering accountability and improving performance.

Exercises

Exercise 1: Identify Key Metrics

1. Choose a recent hiring campaign and list three relevant metrics you could use to evaluate its success.
2. Analyze how each metric contributes to understanding the strengths and weaknesses of the campaign.

Exercise 2: Data-Driven Improvement

1. Select a metric you currently track in your recruitment process.
2. Identify a specific improvement goal, such as reducing time to fill or improving quality of hire.
3. Create an action plan outlining steps you would take to achieve this improvement.

Exercise 3: Building a Recruitment Dashboard

1. Imagine you are building a recruitment dashboard. List five metrics that would be most valuable for monitoring recruitment performance.
2. Describe how you would use this dashboard to make data-driven decisions.

Exercise 4: Diversity and Inclusion Metric Evaluation

1. Assess your organization's diversity metrics and set a target for improving representation in a particular area (e.g., gender, ethnicity).
2. Outline steps you would take to achieve this target, including partnerships, new sourcing channels, or policy adjustments.

Exercise 5: Analyzing Cost per Hire

1. Calculate the cost per hire for a recent recruitment drive, listing all associated costs (e.g., advertising, tools, time).

2. Compare this with the average cost per hire in your industry, identifying any major discrepancies. Suggest cost-saving measures that would bring your costs in line with industry standards.

Conclusion

Talent acquisition metrics and data-driven decision-making offer a strategic advantage in recruiting, providing clear insight into the effectiveness of hiring practices. By focusing on critical metrics, organizations can identify areas for improvement, optimize resource allocation, and support a proactive approach to recruitment. Implementing a metrics-driven strategy helps HR teams not only make informed choices but also demonstrate the value of talent acquisition as a vital contributor to organizational success. As the recruitment landscape continues to evolve, leveraging data will remain essential for attracting, retaining, and developing top talent.

Diversity, Equity & Inclusion (DEI) in Talent Acquisition

Introduction

Diversity, Equity, and Inclusion (DEI) are critical components of a successful talent acquisition strategy. DEI not only enhances workplace culture but also drives innovation, improves employee performance, and better reflects the diverse markets organizations serve. In this chapter, we will explore the importance of DEI in talent acquisition, discuss effective strategies for fostering a diverse workforce, and highlight practical examples and exercises to implement DEI principles in recruitment processes.

Understanding DEI in Talent Acquisition

Diversity refers to the presence of differences within a given setting, including race, ethnicity, gender, age, sexual orientation, disability, and other characteristics.

Equity involves ensuring fair treatment, access, and opportunities for all individuals while striving to identify and eliminate barriers that have historically led to unequal outcomes.

Inclusion is the practice of creating environments in which any individual or group can be and feel welcomed, respected, supported, and valued.

Implementing DEI in talent acquisition goes beyond mere compliance; it signifies a commitment to creating a workplace where everyone has the opportunity to contribute and succeed.

The Business Case for DEI

Investing in DEI within talent acquisition yields numerous benefits for organizations:

- **Enhanced Innovation**: Diverse teams bring varied perspectives, leading to more innovative solutions and improved problem-solving capabilities.

- **Improved Employee Engagement**: Inclusive workplaces foster a sense of belonging, enhancing employee satisfaction and retention rates.

- **Better Financial Performance**: Studies indicate that organizations with diverse leadership are more likely to outperform their peers in terms of profitability.

- **Broader Talent Pool**: Emphasizing DEI allows organizations to tap into a wider array of candidates, enriching their talent pool and improving overall hiring quality.

Example: A leading tech firm implements a DEI initiative and finds that teams with diverse backgrounds develop products that resonate with a broader customer base, ultimately driving sales and market growth.

Strategies for Implementing DEI in Talent Acquisition

1. Assess Current Practices and Metrics

Conduct a comprehensive audit of current talent acquisition practices to identify areas for improvement in diversity, equity, and inclusion. This includes analyzing hiring data, tracking diversity metrics, and evaluating the effectiveness of existing recruitment strategies.

Example: A financial services company conducts an analysis of its hiring data and discovers that women are underrepresented in technical roles. They establish metrics to monitor gender diversity throughout the hiring process, focusing on sourcing, interviewing, and hiring stages.

2. Revise Job Descriptions and Sourcing Strategies

Use inclusive language in job descriptions to attract a diverse range of candidates. Avoid jargon or biased terminology that may discourage applicants from underrepresented groups. Additionally, broaden sourcing strategies to reach diverse candidate pools through targeted outreach efforts.

Example: An advertising agency revamps its job descriptions to focus on essential skills and competencies rather than specific degrees or years of experience, thereby attracting a more diverse range of applicants.

3. Implement Bias-Free Recruitment Practices

Train hiring managers and recruiters to recognize and mitigate unconscious biases during the recruitment process. Standardize interview questions and evaluation criteria to ensure fair assessment of candidates.

Example: A healthcare organization introduces structured interviews, requiring all interviewers to use the same set of standardized questions, reducing the influence of bias on candidate evaluation.

4. Establish Diversity Hiring Goals

Set specific, measurable diversity hiring goals to promote accountability within the organization. These goals should align with the overall strategic objectives of the organization and be regularly reviewed and adjusted.

Example: A technology company sets a goal to increase the percentage of Black and Hispanic employees in engineering roles by 15% over three years, holding recruiting teams accountable for meeting these targets.

5. Leverage Employee Resource Groups (ERGs)

Utilize ERGs to provide insights and support for recruiting diverse talent. ERGs can help identify potential candidates, create inclusive recruitment campaigns, and offer mentorship to underrepresented groups.

Example: A global consulting firm collaborates with its LGBTQ+ ERG to host networking events, which attract diverse candidates and create an inclusive atmosphere for potential hires.

Creating an Inclusive Candidate Experience

Fostering a positive and inclusive candidate experience is crucial for attracting diverse talent. Organizations should focus on the following:

Clear Communication: Maintain open lines of communication with candidates throughout the recruitment process, providing timely updates and feedback.

Welcoming Interviews: Ensure interview panels are diverse and trained in inclusive interviewing practices, creating an environment where candidates feel respected and valued.

Feedback Mechanism: Gather feedback from candidates regarding their experience throughout the recruitment process to identify areas for improvement.

Example: A retail company implements a post-interview survey for candidates, allowing them to share feedback about their experience. This data informs adjustments to the recruitment process, leading to improved candidate satisfaction.

Measuring DEI Success in Talent Acquisition

To gauge the effectiveness of DEI initiatives in talent acquisition, organizations should track and analyze various metrics:

- **Diversity of Applicants**: Monitor the demographics of applicants at each stage of the recruitment process to identify trends and gaps.

- **Hiring Rates**: Evaluate the hiring rates of diverse candidates to assess whether initiatives are effective in attracting and retaining talent.

- **Retention Rates**: Track retention rates of diverse hires to ensure that inclusivity efforts extend beyond recruitment into employee experience and development.

Example: A software development firm analyzes its hiring data and finds that while they attract a diverse applicant pool, their hiring rates for women remain low. This insight prompts a reevaluation of the interview process to ensure it is inclusive and equitable.

Exercises

Exercise 1: Conduct a DEI Audit

1. Evaluate your organization's current talent acquisition practices. Identify three areas where improvements can be made to enhance DEI.
2. Document your findings and propose actionable recommendations for each area.

Exercise 2: Revise a Job Description

1. Choose a job description from your organization that needs revision.
2. Revise it using inclusive language and identify any unnecessary requirements that may limit diverse applicants.

Exercise 3: Create a Candidate Experience Survey

1. Design a survey that assesses the candidate experience during the recruitment process.
2. Include questions that specifically address inclusivity and feedback on interview experiences.

Exercise 4: Set Diversity Hiring Goals

1. Analyze your current workforce demographics and identify an area where diversity is lacking.
2. Set a specific, measurable goal to improve diversity in that area and outline steps to achieve it.

Exercise 5: Develop a Bias-Training Program

1. Outline a training program for hiring managers that addresses unconscious bias in recruitment.
2. Include key topics to cover, training methods, and desired outcomes.

Conclusion

Integrating Diversity, Equity, and Inclusion into talent acquisition is not merely a best practice; it is essential for building a strong, innovative, and effective workforce. By fostering an inclusive recruitment process, organizations can attract and retain diverse talent, ultimately leading to improved performance and a positive workplace culture. Implementing DEI strategies requires commitment, ongoing assessment, and a willingness to adapt, but the rewards are significant—both for employees and the organization as a whole. As talent acquisition continues to evolve, prioritizing DEI will remain a critical driver of success.

Global Talent Acquisition Strategies

Introduction

In today's interconnected world, organizations are increasingly looking beyond their borders to attract the best talent. Global talent acquisition involves not just finding candidates from diverse geographic locations but also understanding local labor markets, cultural differences, and regulatory requirements. This chapter explores the key strategies for successful global talent acquisition, providing insights into navigating the challenges and maximizing the opportunities presented by a global workforce.

The Importance of Global Talent Acquisition

Global talent acquisition offers several benefits:

- **Access to a Wider Talent Pool**: Organizations can tap into a diverse array of skills, experiences, and perspectives that may not be available locally.

- **Increased Innovation**: Diverse teams foster creativity and innovation, driving better business outcomes.

- **Enhanced Competitiveness**: Hiring globally allows organizations to compete effectively in different markets and adapt to regional demands.

- **Flexibility and Resilience**: A geographically diverse workforce can provide greater adaptability in times of crisis, ensuring business continuity.

Example: A multinational technology firm expands its search for software developers beyond the U.S. to include candidates from Europe and Asia. By doing so, they not only fill critical roles faster but also introduce diverse ideas that enhance their product offerings.

Key Strategies for Effective Global Talent Acquisition

1. Understand Local Markets

Each country has its unique labor market dynamics, including cultural norms, salary expectations, and job-seeking behaviors. Organizations must conduct thorough market research to understand these factors, tailoring their recruitment strategies accordingly.

Example: A consumer goods company looking to expand into Southeast Asia invests in market research to understand local recruitment channels. They discover that social media platforms like LinkedIn and local job boards are more effective than traditional methods in attracting candidates.

2. Leverage Technology and Recruitment Tools

Advanced technology can streamline global talent acquisition processes. Utilize applicant tracking systems (ATS), artificial intelligence (AI), and recruitment marketing tools to efficiently manage candidate sourcing, screening, and communication.

Example: A global consulting firm uses AI-driven tools to screen resumes and match candidates with open positions based on their skills and experiences, significantly reducing the time spent on initial candidate evaluations.

3. Build a Strong Employer Brand

A compelling employer brand attracts top talent globally. Organizations should clearly communicate their mission, values, and culture, emphasizing the benefits of working for them across different regions.

Example: An international non-profit organization showcases employee stories on its website and social media, highlighting diverse career paths and the impact of their work, thereby attracting candidates aligned with their mission.

4. Create a Diverse Sourcing Strategy

Utilize multiple sourcing channels to reach diverse candidate pools. This includes leveraging job boards, social media, employee referrals, and partnerships with local organizations that promote diversity.

Example: A healthcare company partners with universities and organizations focused on minority groups to expand its outreach, ensuring a more diverse candidate pool for its nursing roles.

5. Foster a Culturally Inclusive Recruitment Process

Train hiring managers and recruiters on cultural competencies to ensure an inclusive hiring process. Understanding cultural differences can enhance the candidate experience and promote a positive employer brand.

Example: A financial services firm provides cultural sensitivity training for its recruitment team, enabling them to engage effectively with candidates from different backgrounds, ultimately improving candidate satisfaction and acceptance rates.

Navigating Compliance and Regulatory Requirements

When hiring globally, organizations must navigate various compliance and regulatory requirements, including employment laws, visa regulations, and tax implications. It's essential to understand these legal aspects to avoid costly mistakes and ensure a smooth hiring process.

Example: A technology company looking to hire engineers in India partners with a local HR consultancy to navigate the complexities of labor laws and ensure compliance with hiring practices, minimizing legal risks.

Global Onboarding Strategies

Effective onboarding is crucial for integrating new hires into a global organization. A structured onboarding program should encompass cultural orientation, compliance training, and job-specific training to facilitate smooth transitions for international employees.

Example: A multinational corporation implements a global onboarding program that includes virtual orientation sessions, mentorship programs, and language support for international hires, enhancing their onboarding experience.

Measuring Success in Global Talent Acquisition

To evaluate the effectiveness of global talent acquisition strategies, organizations should track key performance indicators (KPIs) such as:

- **Time to Fill**: Monitor the average time taken to fill positions across different regions to identify bottlenecks.

- **Quality of Hire**: Assess the performance and retention rates of hires in various locations to gauge the effectiveness of sourcing and selection processes.

- **Diversity Metrics**: Track the diversity of applicants and hires across different markets to ensure inclusivity goals are met.

Example: A multinational retail company evaluates its global talent acquisition strategy by analyzing time-to-fill and diversity metrics, enabling them to make informed adjustments to their recruitment processes.

Challenges in Global Talent Acquisition

Despite the opportunities, global talent acquisition comes with challenges, including:

- **Cultural Differences**: Understanding and adapting to diverse workplace cultures can be challenging for organizations and may affect candidate experience.
- **Regulatory Complexity**: Navigating different employment laws and compliance requirements can be cumbersome.
- **Competition for Talent**: In some regions, competition for skilled talent is intense, making it essential to differentiate the organization's offerings.

Exercises

Exercise 1: Market Research Assessment

1. Choose a target country for global talent acquisition. Conduct market research to identify key factors such as salary expectations, prevalent recruitment channels, and cultural norms.
2. Present your findings and suggest tailored recruitment strategies based on the local market.

Exercise 2: Employer Brand Development

1. Develop a brief employer branding strategy for your organization aimed at attracting international candidates.
2. Include key messages, target audiences, and channels to promote your brand globally.

Exercise 3: Compliance Checklist

1. Create a compliance checklist that outlines key employment laws and regulations for a specific country where you plan to hire talent.

2. Discuss potential challenges and solutions for navigating these regulations.

Exercise 4: Global Onboarding Plan

1. Design an onboarding plan for new hires in different regions, considering cultural, legal, and job-specific requirements.
2. Outline key components of the plan and how you will ensure a consistent and inclusive onboarding experience.

Exercise 5: Analyze Global Recruitment KPIs\

1. Identify three KPIs relevant to global talent acquisition and explain why they are important.
2. Outline a plan for how you would collect and analyze data for these KPIs to measure recruitment success.

Conclusion

Global talent acquisition is a strategic imperative for organizations seeking to thrive in a competitive marketplace. By understanding local markets, leveraging technology, building a strong employer brand, and fostering an inclusive recruitment process, organizations can effectively navigate the complexities of hiring globally. Emphasizing compliance and implementing robust onboarding strategies further enhance the candidate experience, ensuring successful integration into the organization. As businesses continue to operate on a global scale, prioritizing effective talent acquisition strategies will be essential for sustained growth and success.

Acquiring Passive Talent

Introduction

In today's competitive job market, many of the best candidates are not actively seeking new employment. These passive candidates—those currently employed and not openly looking for new opportunities—represent a significant talent pool that organizations can tap into. This chapter explores the strategies and techniques for effectively acquiring passive talent, emphasizing the importance of building relationships and creating compelling engagement tactics.

Understanding Passive Talent

Passive candidates are individuals who are currently employed and may not be actively searching for a new job but could be open to new opportunities if approached effectively. They often possess the skills and experience that organizations seek, making them valuable assets for recruitment efforts. Engaging with passive talent requires a different approach compared to traditional recruitment methods, focusing on relationship-building rather than immediate placements.

Example: A leading software company identifies a top-performing engineer at a competitor's firm. While this engineer is not looking for a new job, the company initiates a conversation about potential opportunities, showcasing their innovative projects and work culture, sparking the engineer's interest.

The Importance of Acquiring Passive Talent
Acquiring passive talent offers several advantages:

- **Access to High-Quality Candidates**: Passive candidates often have a proven track record of success in their current roles, making them highly desirable.

- **Reduced Competition**: Engaging with passive candidates allows organizations to tap into talent pools that may not be actively pursued by other companies.

- **Improved Retention Rates**: Candidates who are approached thoughtfully and presented with compelling opportunities are more likely to feel valued and engaged, leading to higher retention rates.

Example: A healthcare organization recruits a nurse who is content in their current position but intrigued by the potential for career growth and professional development. By presenting a tailored opportunity, the organization successfully attracts this passive candidate, enhancing its workforce.

Strategies for Acquiring Passive Talent

1. Build a Strong Employer Brand

Creating a compelling employer brand is essential for attracting passive candidates. Showcase your organization's culture, values, and success stories through various channels, including social media, company websites, and employee testimonials. A strong employer brand can pique the interest of passive candidates who may not be actively job hunting.

Example: A global consulting firm shares regular updates on its projects and employee achievements on LinkedIn, highlighting its inclusive work environment and opportunities for advancement, drawing the attention of passive candidates in their industry.

2. Leverage Social Media and Professional Networks
Utilize social media platforms like LinkedIn, Twitter, and industry-specific forums to identify and connect with passive candidates. Engage in conversations, share valuable content, and participate in discussions to build relationships and establish credibility within your target talent pool.

Example: A marketing agency identifies potential candidates by joining industry-related LinkedIn groups. By contributing to discussions and sharing insights, they position themselves as thought leaders, which attracts passive candidates' interest.

3. Use Employee Referrals

Encourage current employees to refer passive candidates from their networks. Employees often have connections with skilled professionals who may not be actively seeking new roles but would consider opportunities if approached. Incentivizing referrals can motivate employees to engage their networks.

Example: A tech company implements an employee referral program that rewards employees for introducing potential candidates, leading to the successful recruitment of several passive talents who were previously unaware of the company's openings.

4. Create Talent Pools

Establish and maintain a database of potential candidates, including passive talent. Regularly engage with these candidates through newsletters, industry insights, and personalized communications to keep them informed about your organization and potential opportunities.

Example: A finance company builds a talent pool of qualified analysts who showed interest in previous job openings but were not selected. By maintaining regular contact and providing updates about the company's growth and opportunities, they keep these candidates warm for future roles.

5. Personalized Outreach

When reaching out to passive candidates, personalize your communication. Highlight specific skills or experiences that make them a great fit for your organization and provide a compelling reason for them to consider a conversation.

Example: A pharmaceutical company identifies a research scientist with a strong publication record. They reach out with a personalized message that references specific projects the scientist has worked on and how their expertise aligns with the company's current initiatives.

Creating a Positive Candidate Experience

When engaging with passive candidates, it's vital to create a positive and respectful experience. This includes clear communication about the recruitment process, timely follow-ups, and genuine appreciation for their time and interest.

Example: A retail organization schedules an initial conversation with a passive candidate and follows up promptly, providing feedback on the discussion. This respect for the candidate's time fosters a positive impression and keeps the door open for future engagement.

Measuring Success in Acquiring Passive Talent

To evaluate the effectiveness of passive talent acquisition strategies, organizations should track relevant metrics, such as:

- **Response Rates**: Monitor the percentage of passive candidates who respond positively to outreach efforts.

- **Conversion Rates**: Assess how many engaged passive candidates progress to interviews and ultimately receive job offers.

- **Retention Rates**: Track the retention rates of hired passive candidates to measure long-term success and engagement.

Example: A digital marketing agency evaluates its outreach efforts by analyzing response rates and conversion rates for passive candidates. By refining their messaging based on feedback, they improve their success in attracting and hiring top talent.

Challenges in Acquiring Passive Talent

Acquiring passive talent presents several challenges:

- **Time-Intensive Process**: Engaging passive candidates often requires more time and effort compared to sourcing active candidates.

- **Relationship Building**: Establishing rapport with passive candidates can be challenging, especially when they are content in their current roles.

- **Competition for Talent**: Many organizations are competing for the same pool of passive candidates, making differentiation crucial.

Exercises

Exercise 1: Develop an Employer Branding Strategy

1. Outline a strategy for enhancing your organization's employer brand to attract passive candidates.
2. Include key messages, target audiences, and platforms for promotion.

Exercise 2: Create a Social Media Engagement Plan

1. Design a plan for leveraging social media to engage with passive candidates in your industry.
2. Identify specific content types, posting schedules, and engagement tactics.

Exercise 3: Build a Talent Pool

1. Create a framework for establishing a talent pool of passive candidates, including criteria for selection and methods for engagement.
2. Discuss how you would maintain relationships with these candidates over time.

Exercise 4: Personal Outreach Template

1. Draft a personalized outreach message for a passive candidate in your industry.
2. Highlight what makes the candidate a good fit and what opportunities your organization can offer.

Exercise 5: Analyze Outreach Metrics

1. Identify three metrics to track the effectiveness of your passive talent acquisition efforts.
2. Develop a plan for how you would collect and analyze this data to improve your strategy.

Conclusion

Acquiring passive talent is a strategic approach that can significantly enhance an organization's recruitment efforts. By building a strong employer brand, leveraging social media, utilizing employee referrals, and creating positive candidate experiences, organizations can successfully engage with passive candidates. Measuring success through relevant metrics allows for continuous improvement in strategies, ensuring that organizations remain competitive in attracting top talent. As the job market evolves, understanding and effectively reaching out to passive talent will be essential for sustained success in talent acquisition.

Talent Acquisition Case Studies and Exercises

Introduction

Understanding successful talent acquisition strategies requires real-world examples that illustrate effective practices and common challenges. This chapter presents a collection of case studies showcasing diverse organizations and their innovative approaches to talent acquisition. Accompanying exercises will help you apply these insights to your own organization, enabling you to refine and enhance your recruitment processes.

Case Study 1: Google's Innovative Recruitment Process

Google is renowned for its rigorous and innovative recruitment strategies, which focus on attracting top talent while maintaining a strong company culture. The company utilizes a data-driven approach, leveraging analytics to identify the characteristics of successful employees.

Key Strategies:

- **Structured Interviews**: Google uses structured interviews to ensure consistency and objectivity in the evaluation process. Candidates are assessed based on predetermined criteria that align with job requirements and organizational values.

- **Work Sample Tests**: The company employs work sample tests that simulate real job tasks, allowing candidates to demonstrate their skills and problem-solving abilities in a practical context.

Outcome: Google's approach has led to a more diverse and talented workforce, with significant improvements in employee performance and retention rates.

Example Exercise:

1. Analyze your current recruitment process. Identify areas where structured interviews or work sample tests could be implemented.
2. Develop a plan for integrating these methods into your hiring process, including criteria for evaluation.

Case Study 2: Unilever's Digital Recruitment Strategy

Unilever faced challenges in attracting young talent and streamlining its recruitment process. To address this, the company adopted a digital recruitment strategy that leveraged technology to enhance candidate experience and engagement.

Key Strategies:

- **Gamification**: Unilever introduced gamified assessments that allow candidates to showcase their skills in an engaging and interactive manner. This approach not only attracts young talent but also provides insights into candidates' problem-solving capabilities and cultural fit.

- **AI-Powered Screening**: The company implemented AI algorithms to screen resumes and analyze candidate responses, reducing time spent on initial evaluations and ensuring a more diverse candidate pool.

Outcome: Unilever's innovative approach has led to a significant increase in application rates from millennials and Gen Z candidates, along with improved quality of hires.

Example Exercise:

1. Explore ways to incorporate gamification into your recruitment process. Identify specific roles or assessments where this could be beneficial.

2. Create a prototype for a gamified assessment relevant to your industry.

Case Study 3: Starbucks' Commitment to Diversity and Inclusion

Starbucks is committed to fostering a diverse workforce and creating an inclusive culture. The company actively works to recruit from various demographics, ensuring representation across all levels of the organization.

Key Strategies:
- **Partnerships with Diverse Organizations**: Starbucks collaborates with community organizations and educational institutions to create pipelines for underrepresented groups.
- **Diversity Training for Recruiters**: The company provides diversity and inclusion training for its recruitment teams to mitigate biases and promote inclusive hiring practices.

Outcome: Starbucks has seen a notable increase in the diversity of its workforce, leading to enhanced innovation and customer engagement.

Example Exercise:
1. Assess your organization's current diversity recruitment strategies. Identify potential partnerships with organizations that promote diversity.
2. Develop a diversity training program outline for your recruitment team.

Case Study 4: IBM's Global Talent Acquisition Framework

IBM recognized the need for a cohesive global talent acquisition strategy to effectively compete in various markets. The company implemented a unified framework that emphasizes local adaptations within a global strategy.

Key Strategies:
- **Centralized Recruitment Platform**: IBM established a centralized recruitment platform that allows local teams

to customize job postings and recruitment approaches while adhering to global brand standards.
- **Local Talent Acquisition Specialists**: The company employs local talent acquisition specialists who understand regional markets and cultural nuances, ensuring effective engagement with candidates.

Outcome: IBM's global framework has led to improved efficiency in hiring processes, enhanced candidate experience, and a better understanding of local talent markets.

Example Exercise:

1. Evaluate your organization's talent acquisition strategy. Identify areas where a centralized framework could be beneficial.
2. Develop a proposal for establishing local talent acquisition teams within a centralized structure.

Exercises for Skill Development

Exercise 1: Analyze a Recruitment Campaign

1. Choose a recent recruitment campaign from a well-known organization. Analyze its strategies, messaging, and channels used for outreach.
2. Present your findings and discuss what elements could be applied to your organization's recruitment efforts.

Exercise 2: Create a Candidate Persona

1. Develop a candidate persona for a critical role in your organization. Include demographics, skills, motivations, and preferred communication channels.
2. Use this persona to design a targeted recruitment strategy that addresses the specific needs and preferences of this candidate group.

Exercise 3: Evaluate Recruitment Metrics

1. Identify three key metrics currently used in your recruitment process. Analyze their effectiveness and relevance.
2. Propose additional metrics that could provide deeper insights into your talent acquisition efforts, such as candidate satisfaction or diversity ratios.

Exercise 4: Develop a Recruitment Marketing Plan

1. Create a recruitment marketing plan that outlines how your organization will promote its employer brand and attract talent.
2. Include specific channels, messaging strategies, and key performance indicators (KPIs) for measuring success.

Exercise 5: Design an Onboarding Program

1. Design an onboarding program for new hires that aligns with your organization's culture and values.
2. Incorporate elements that will help integrate new employees into the team and ensure a smooth transition into their roles.

Conclusion

Talent acquisition is an evolving discipline that requires organizations to continuously adapt and innovate. By examining case studies of successful companies, organizations can glean valuable insights into effective strategies and practices. The accompanying exercises provide practical applications to enhance your talent acquisition efforts, ultimately contributing to a more effective recruitment process. As you implement these strategies, remember that flexibility and responsiveness to changing market dynamics are key to achieving sustained success in talent acquisition.

www.ingramcontent.com/pod-product-compliance
Lightning Source LLC
Chambersburg PA
CBHW030035230526
45472CB00002B/516